MORE
MAKING OUT
IN
JAPANESE

What the critics said about *Making Out in Japanese:*

" . . . dangerous . . . "
—*Mainichi Daily News*

" . . . dangerous . . . "
—*Daily Yomiuri*

" . . . dangerous . . . "
—*Japan Times*

MORE
MAKING OUT IN JAPANESE

by
Todd & Erika Geers
illustrations by Erika Geers

YENBOOKS

To Elisha

YENBOOKS are published and distributed
by the Charles E. Tuttle Company, Inc.
with editorial offices at
2-6 Suido 1-chome, Bunkyo-ku, Tokyo 112, Japan

Library of Congress Catalog Card No. 89-51323
International Standard Book No. 0-8048-1592-5

First edition 1990
Seventh printing, 1991

Printed in Japan

CONTENTS

INTRODUCTION

So how's your Japanese coming along? Are you now conversing effortlessly? No? Still don't know what they're talking about sometimes? Sounds like you didn't read *Making Out in Japanese*. So go out and buy a copy—over 50,000 other people have. Read it, study it, live it, and love it. *Making Out in Japanese* will show you how the Japanese *really* speak. We use lots of shortcuts in our speech, and so do they. Our colloquial way of speaking is relaxed and informal, and so is theirs. OK, with that plug out of the way, let's move on to some new stuff.

In Japanese there is a slang use of "A," "B," and "C" similar to the American English slang use of "first base," "second base," "third base," and "home run." These letters denote kissing, petting, and making love, respectively. The focus of this book is love, and the words and phrases in it are listed in "love groups" corresponding to these activities. In Chapter 1, "Kissing," you'll find all the words and phrases you'll need to string and fire Cupid's bow. Chapter 2, "Petting," will get you into a little more intimate action, but it's rather tame compared with Chapter 3, "Making Love." If your relationship should deteriorate before reaching Chapter 3, then Chapter 4, "Fighting," is the one for you. But if you hear wedding bells ringing, head for Chapter 5, "Marriage." Finally, don't forget Chapter 6, "Health." All those activities in Chapters 1 through 5 are more fun if you're in (or can get into) good shape.

INFORMATION

It's rather difficult to teach the proper pronunciation of a foreign language in a book, so we're not going to try. To help you out, though, we've joined two and sometimes three or four words together, to make compound words or phrases that are easier to pronounce. Most of these compounds are hyphenated to highlight merged words, to emphasize the slang suffixes and particles, and to facilitate pronunciation and memorization. *Fuzakenai-deyo,* for example, is a compound phrase meaning "Don't be stupid!" Its components are: *fuzake* (from *fuzakeru*), *nai* *(arimasen),* and the slang suffix *-deyo*. The compound phrase is rendered *fuzakenai-deyo* so that you will not pause while pronouncing it, but say it entirely in one breath; a pause in the pronunciation will make the impact weaker.

We're sure that you're familiar with the interrogative sentence forms *desu-ka* and *masu-ka*. Forget them. Except for a few still employed when talking to strangers, requesting services, etc., the rest have been dismissed. In informal speech, rising intonation takes the place of these forms. Thus, the final syllables of all words and phrases in this book ending with a question mark should be pronounced with the kind of rising intonation we give to the question "Right?"

The terms "boy" and "girl" are used throughout the

9

book. Here, we are definitely referring to the sexes in the post-puberty phase. Still, these sound a bit cuter than "man" and "woman." If there's one thing you must understand to make it in the world of Japanese romance, it's the power of "cute." Suppose, for example, you don't know how to play tennis. It's not really important because, come the spring, you must, like all the style-conscious Japanese, carry a tennis racket everywhere you go. It's not important whether or how well you play. What's important is that you have a cute cover for your racket, preferably with three Mickey Mouse patches and some English words. (Note: the English should *not* make sense—something like "Active Sports: Traditional Mind for Specialty" would do nicely.)

To eliminate the embarrassing problem of boys using girls' words or vice versa, we've indicated the words suitable for use by girls and boys with the symbols ♀ and ♂ respectively. A word designated ♂ ♀ can be used by both sexes. For example:

Don't be upset.	*Okoranaide.* ♀
	Okoruna-yo. ♂
Make me warm.	*Atatamete.* ♂ ♀

There are two ways to say *ne:* the short *ne (ne),* said with a falling intonation to show agreement or to add friendliness to speech; and the long *ne (nē),* said with a rising intonation, often soliciting agreement with the meaning of "Isn't it?" or "Aren't you?" Girls prefer *ne* and *nē* to convey these meanings; guys prefer *na* and *nā.* But if the guys wish to upgrade their speech, they should use *ne* and *nē,* especially when talking to girls.

Slang that is too faddish is not included in this book, because such words come and go too quickly. If you use old slang, the reaction of your Japanese date will likely be "He thinks he's being cool speaking like that, but nobody says that anymore. Hah, hah!" So avoid the hot slang—if it's out of date people will think that you're funny or square.

The Japanese have been borrowing foreign words for so long that they've invented a special syllabary, *katakana,* just to spell them with. Many of these loanwords appear in this book. (To help you spot them, they're printed in bold.) For example, to tell a girl "I like your hairstyle," you could say *Kimi-no* **heasutairu** *suki.* The Japanese language has only one final consonant (n), so when Japanese pronounce English words with consonant endings, they often tack on a vowel. The word "back," for example, becomes **bakku;** "cute" becomes **kyūto;** "game" becomes **gēmu.** The final "r" sound, also, does not exist in Japanese. This ending is usually replaced with a long "a" sound when pronounced by Japanese. The word "locker," for example, becomes **rokkā.** And since there is no English "l" sound in Japanese, an "r" is used in its place. Japanese enjoy using English words sporadically in their speech and you should do the same. With a little practice, it's easy to get the hang of how to "*katakana*-ize" an English word, that is, to pronounce it the way a Japanese would.

Now, shall we get on first base?

KISSING

1

Have I seen you before?	*Mae-ni atta-koto aru?* ♂♀
Do you come here often?	*Koko-ni yoku kuru?* ♂♀
You come here often, don't you?	*Koko-ni yoku kuru-deshō?* ♂♀ *Koko-ni yoku kuru-darō?* ♂
I've been watching you.	*Anata-no-koto zutto miteta.* ♀ *Kimi-no-koto zutto miteta.* ♂
You're really pretty.	*Kimi-tte hontō-ni kirei-dane.* ♂
You're handsome.	*Anata-tte **hansamu**-ne.* ♀
You're fascinating.	*Anata-wa miryokuteki-ne.* ♀ *Kimi-wa miryokuteki-da.* ♂

13

I want to know more about you.	*Anata-ni-tsuite motto shiritai.* ♀ *Kimi-ni-tsuite motto shiritai.* ♂
Come on, tell me more.	*Ii-janai. Motto oshiete-yo.* ♂ ♀
Don't be shy.	*Hazukashigaranaide.** ♂ ♀

*Also means "Don't be embarrassed."

Ask me some questions.	*Nanka shitsumon-shite.* ♂ ♀ *Nanka kiite.* ♂ ♀
Ask me anything you want.	*Suki-na-koto nandemo kiite ii-no-yo.* ♀ *Suki-na-koto nandemo kiite-ii-yo.* ♂ ♀
Except what color underwear I'm wearing.	*Nani iro-no shitagi-kawa dame.* ♂ ♀

I like your personality. *Anata-no seikaku suki-yo.* ♀
Kimi-no seikaku suki-dayo. ♂

You're my type. *Anata-wa atashi-no suki-na* **taipu**. ♀
Kimi-wa boku-no suki-na **taipu**. ♂

What's your type? *Donna hito-ga suki?* ♂ ♀
Donna hito-ga konomi? ♂ ♀

quiet: *otonashii* (usually said about girls)
mukuchi-na (usually said about boys)
loud: *nigiyaka-na*
funny: *omoshiroi*
serious: *majime-na*
big: *ōkii*
small: *chiisai*
considerate: *omoiyari-no aru*
bright: *akarui*
tender: *yasashii*
manly: *otokoppoi*
feminine: *onnappoi*
cheerful: *genki-no aru*
smart: *atama-no ii*
cute: *kawaii*
sexy: **sekushii**-na
slim: *yaseteru*

chubby: *potchari-shita*
glamorous: **guramā**-na
thin-waisted: **uesto**-ga hosoi
small butt: *chiisai oshiri-no*
long hair: *kami-no nagai*
cute smile: *egao-no kawaii*
pretty teeth: *ha-no kirei-na*
small breasts: *mune-no chiisai*
rich: *okane-mochi-no*
tough: **tafu**-na
elite: **erīto**-na
stylish: **sutairisshu**-na
shy: *hazukashigari-ya*
outgoing: *shitashimi-no aru*
long legs: *ashi-no nagai*
big eyes: *me-ga ōkii*
small mouth: *kuchi-no chiisai*
sporty: **supōti**-na

Substitute the words above in the following sentence:

I like _____ type of person.

_____ *hito-ga ii.* ♂ ♀

I like your hairstyle.

Anata-no **hea sutairu** *suki.* ♀
Kimi-no **hea sutairu** *suki.* ♂

Do you follow the latest fads?

Ryūkō-o ou? ♂ ♀

What's in now?

Nani-ga ima hayatteru-no? ♂ ♀

You have good taste in clothes.

*Fuku-no konomi-ga ii-ne.** ♀
*Fuku-no konomi-ga ii-na.** ♂

Konomi can be replaced with *shumi.*

...t very stylish.

Atashi-wa ryūkō-ni binkan-ja nai. ♀
*Atashi-wa anmari **sutairisshu**-ja nai.** ♀
Boku-wa ryūkō-ni binkan-ja nai. ♂
*Boku-wa anmari **sutairisshu**-ja nai.** ♂

*Especially said about clothes.

Will you give me some advice?

*Nanika **adobaisu**-shitekureru?* ♂ ♀

Shall we go shopping together someday?

*Kondo issho-ni **shoppingu**-ni ikanai?* ♂ ♀

I don't like to shop alone.

*Hitori-de **shoppingu**-suru-nowa suki-ja nai.* ♂ ♀

Do you have a steady?

Tsukiatteru hito iru? ♂ ♀

You must be very popular.	*Moteru-deshō.* ♂ ♀ *Moteru-darō.* ♂
You must have many boyfriends/girlfriends. (You must be popular.)	*Kanojo ippai irun-deshō.* ♀ *Kareshi ippai irun-darō.* ♂
You must have a girl-friend/boyfriend.	*Kanojo irun-deshō.** ♀ *Kareshi irun-darō.** ♂

*The nuance is "You are pretty/handsome; therefore, I think you must have a steady." Use these phrases to check if the person has a steady without coming right out and asking.

Yes, I had one, but we just broke up.	*Un demo, saikin wakare-ta.* ♂ ♀
I've never dated a Japanese boy/girl before.	*Nihon-no otoko-no-hito-to **dēto**-shita-koto-nai.* ♀ *Nihon-no onna-no-hito-to **dēto**-shita-koto-nai.* ♂
Will you go out with me?	*Atashi-to dekakenai?* ♀ *Boku-to dekakenai?* ♂
I don't have anyone to share ice cream with.	*Atashi-wa **aisu kurīmu**-o issho-ni taberu hito-ga inai-no.* ♀ *Boku-wa **aisu kurīmu**-o issho-ni taberu hito-ga inain-da.** ♂

*Japanese girls love ice cream. This should get a date for the boy.

Do you smoke?	*Tabako* suu? ♂ ♀
Do you drink beer/liquor/wine?	*Biiru/osake/wain* nomu? ♂ ♀
What do/did you study at college?	*Daigaku-de nani-o senkō-shiteru-no?* ♂ ♀ *Daigaku-de nani-o senkō-shita-no?* ♂ ♀

*Senkō means "major study area."

I went to a special (trade) school.	*Atashi-wa senmon gakkō-ni itta.* ♀ *Boku-wa senmon gakkō-ni itta.* ♂
What type of school?	*Donna gakkō?* ♂ ♀
Allow us to introduce ourselves.	*Atashitachi-no jikoshōkai-sasete.* ♀ *Bokutachi-no jikoshōkai-sasete.* ♂

Would you introduce your friends?	*Anata-no tomodachi-o shōkai-shite?* ♀ *Kimi-no tomodachi-o shōkai-shite?* ♂
Let's move to a bigger table.	*Motto ōkii **tēburu**-ni utsurō.* ♂ ♀
Let's pair off.	*Kōgo-ni suwarō.*[1] ♂ ♀ *Ittai itchi-ni wakareyō.*[2] ♂ ♀

*1. To sit down in pairs.
*2. Separate and go do something as couples.

What do you think about this?	*Kore-ni tsuite dō omou?* ♂ ♀
You don't talk very much.	*Anata-wa anmari shaberanai-none.* ♀ *Kimi-wa anmari shaberanai-ne.* ♂
What do your friends want to do?	*Anata-no tomodachi nani-ga shitai-no?* ♀ *Kimi-no tomodachi nani-ga shitai-no?* ♂
Let's all go out together.	*Minna-de dekakeyō.*[1] ♂ ♀ *Minna-de deyō.*[2] ♂ ♀

*1. Making plans to go out.
*2. As in "Let's leave this building."

It'll be a lot of fun.	*Zettai tanoshii-yo.* ♂ ♀
Let's go to the beach.	*Umi-ni ikō.* ♂ ♀
Let's see a movie.	*Eiga-o miyō.* ♂ ♀
Who is your favorite actor/actress?	*Yakusha/Joyū -de dare-ga suki?** ♂ ♀

*Yakusha means both actor and actress, and *joyū* means only actress.

Did you see _____?	_____ *mita?* ♂ ♀
I like _____.	_____-*ga suki.* ♂ ♀

Japanese are fond of onomatopoeias, words that imitate sounds. Used at the right moment, the following "sound words" will produce a laugh or three.

dog barking	*wan-wan* ♂ ♀
cat meowing	*nyan-nyan* ♂ ♀
heavy rain	*zā-zā* ♂ ♀
light rain	*shito-shito* ♂ ♀
walking noise	*teku-teku* ♂ ♀
heavy crying	*en-en* ♂ ♀
light crying	*shiku-shiku** ♂ ♀

*Rub your eyes while saying *shiku-shiku*.

I'm hungry.	*Onaka-ga peko-peko.* ♂ ♀
My head feels dizzy.	*Atama-ga fura-fura.* ♂ ♀
I have a sharp pain in my stomach.	*Onaka-ga kiri-kiri itai.* ♂ ♀
What time does the next show start?	*Tsugi-no kai nanji (desu-ka)?* ♂ ♀
We have plenty of time.	*Takusan jikan-ga aru.* ♂ ♀ *Jikan-ga ippai aru.* ♂ ♀

Let's make a line. (Let's get in line.)	*Narabō.* ♂ ♀
Are you waiting in line?	*Naranderun desu-ka?* ♂ ♀ *Naranderu-no?* ♂ ♀
You wait here.	*Koko-de mattete.* ♂ ♀
I'll do/buy it.	*Atashi-ga suru-wa/kau-wa.* ♀ *Boku-ga suru-yo/kau-yo.* ♂
Let's sing *karaoke*.	*Karaoke-de utaō.* ♂ ♀

NOTE: *Karaoke* literally means "without orchestra." This popular activity usually takes place in special *karaoke* bars, and consists of individual patrons singing the vocal lead of favorite songs, to the accompaniment of taped backup instrumentals. Like all their fun, Japanese take this very seriously.

Do you like *karaoke*?	*Karaoke suki?* ♂ ♀

That person's singing is interesting.	*Ano hito-no utaikata omoshiroi.* ♂ ♀
What's a popular thing to do?	*Nani-ga hayatteru-no?* ♂ ♀
Let's go to Yamashita Park.	*Yamashita **Pāku**-e ikō.* ♂ ♀
I hear it's a good spot for a date.	***Dēto-spotto**-datte kiita.* ♂ ♀
Let's go to the park again.	*Mata **pāku**/kōen -ni ikō.* ♂ ♀
I love to hold your hand as we walk through the park.	*Anata-to te-o tsunaide kōen-o aruku-noga suki-yo.* ♀ *Kimi-to te-o tsunaide kōen-o aruku-noga suki-dayo.* ♂
I came here by car.	*Kuruma-de kita.* ♂ ♀
Would you like to go for a drive?	***Doraibu**-ni ikitai?* ♂ ♀
I have room for two of your friends.	*Anata-no tomodachi futari-bun-no seki-mo aru-wayo.* ♀ *Kimi-no tomodachi futari-bun-no seki-mo aru-yo.* * ♂

*Sure way to get her to go.

I'll order (for you/us).	*Ōdā-shite ageru.* ♂ ♀
Would you like something to eat/drink?	*Nanika taberu/nomu?* ♂ ♀
What do you want?	*Nani-ga ii?* ♂ ♀
Let's go Dutch.	*Warikan-ni shiyō.* ♂ ♀
Let's have one check.	*Denpyō-o issho-ni shiyō.* ♂ ♀
One check, please.	*Denpyō-o hitotsu-ni shite kudasai.* ♂ ♀

Which credit cards do you accept?	*Doko-no* **kurejitto kādo**-*ga tsukaemasu-ka?* ♂ ♀
I lost my wallet.	*Saifu-o nakushita.* ♂ ♀
I don't have any money.	*Okane-ga nanimo-nai.* ♂ ♀
Can I borrow 10,000 yen?	*Ichiman-en kashite-kureru?* ♂ ♀
I scored (with her).	*Nampa-shita.** ♂

> **Nampa* means "dishonest person" and the opposite, *kōha*, means "honest person." A *nampa* person might ask to make love on the first date, whereas a *kōha* person might wait till their wedding night. In this context, *Nampa-shita* means "I went girl hunting (successfully)." This is a boy's phrase because only girls get *nampa*'d. A *nampa-yarō* is a boy who likes girl hunting. (*Kōha-shita* does not have any meaning.)

Drink up!	*Ikki! Ikki!** ♂ ♀

> **Ikki! Ikki!* is an encouraging cheer which means something like "Drink it all up without stopping."

Cheers!	*Kampai!** ♂ ♀

> **Kampai!* is said as everyone is clinking their glasses together for the toast. It means, literally, "dry glass."

Drink quickly to catch up.	*Kaketsuke ippai.* ♂ ♀
I'm getting drunk.	*Yotte-kichatta.* ♂ ♀ *Yopparatte-kichatta.* ♂ ♀

I'm drunk.	*Yotchatta.* ♂ ♀ *Yopparatchatta.* ♂ ♀
I have a splitting headache.	*Atama-ga wareru-yō-ni itai.* ♂ ♀ *Sugoi zutsū-ga suru.* ♂ ♀
You drank too much last night, didn't you?	*Kinō-wa takusan nomisugita-nē?* ♂ ♀ *Kinō-wa takusan nomisugita-nā?* ♂
By the way, . . .	*Tokorode, . . .* ♂ ♀
I'm sorry, but . . .	*Warui-kedo, . . .* ♂ ♀
Who was that?	*Are dare?* ♂ ♀

Will you be my Japanese teacher?	*Atashi-no nihongo-no sensei-ni nattekureru?* ♀ *Boku-no nihongo-no sensei-ni nattekureru?* ♂
I'll teach you English.	*Atashi-ga eigo-o oshiete ageru.* ♀ *Boku-ga eigo-o oshiete ageru.* ♂
What shall we do now?	*Ima-kara dō-suru?* ♂ ♀
I want to go to _____.	*_____-ni ikitai.* ♂ ♀
I'm lost.	*Michi-ni mayotta.*[1] ♂ ♀ *Wakaranai.*[2] ♂ ♀

[1]. This is used when you've lost your way.
[2]. This is used when you don't understand.

Please write down the directions for me.	*Iki-kata-o kaite.* ♂ ♀
Don't forget to list the train station names.	*Eki-no namae-no **risuto**-o wasurenaide.* ♂ ♀
Will you tell me which train to take?	*Dotchi-no densha-ka oshietekureru?* ♂ ♀
How will I know when to get off (the train)?	*Itsu oriru-ka dō wakaru-no?* ♂ ♀
I'll be waiting at _____.	_____ *-de matteru.* ♂ ♀
Get off at _____ (station).	_____ *(eki)-de orite.** ♂ ♀

*Eki, which means "station," is added to the proper name of some stations, but not to all: e.g., Yokohama Eki, Kanagawa Shinmachi, etc.

Are you busy right now?

Ima isogashii? ♂ ♀

Let's go to a disco.

Disuko*-ni ikō. ♂ ♀

Let's go to your favorite disco.

*Anata-no yoku iku **disuko**-ni ikō.*** ♀
*Kimi-no yoku iku **disuko**-ni ikō.* ♂

*Use *yoku iku* to describe a place you "go to often."

I've never been to a disco.

*Mada **disuko**-ni itta-koto-nai.* ♂ ♀

Is it true Japanese boys dance together?

Nihon-no otoko-no-hito-tte issho-ni odorutte honto? ♂ ♀

How much is the admission?

Hairu-no ikura? ♂ ♀

Does it include food and drink?

Tabemono-to nomimono komi? ♂ ♀

Do we get membership cards?

Menbāshippu kādo*-wa moraemasu-ka? ♂ ♀

*Said to club staff. When talking to friends, use the less formal *moraeru?*

I'm a member.

*Atashi-wa **menbā** (desu).* ♀
*Boku-wa **menbā** (desu).* ♂

Here are your tickets.	*Hai, **chiketto**.* ♂ ♀
	Hai-yo.* ♂ ♀
	Hora-yo.* ♂

*Hai-yo and *Hora-yo* mean "Here you go" as one might say when handing over something.

Are there lockers here?	***Rokkā** arimasu-ka?* ♂ ♀
	***Rokkā** aru?* ♂ ♀
Let's use the lockers.	***Rokkā**-o tsukaō.* ♂ ♀
Where do you want to sit?	*Doko-ni suwaritai?* ♂ ♀
It's noisy here.	*Koko urusai.* ♂ ♀
It's too noisy here.	*Koko urusasugiru.* ♂ ♀

There's too much "traffic" here.	*Hitodōri-ga ōsugiru.* * ♂ ♀

    *Hitodōri applies to "people traffic" only.

It's dark over there.	*Asoko-wa kurai.* ♂ ♀
These seats look good.	*Kono isu yosasō.* ♂ ♀
This is a nonsmoking section.	*Koko-wa kin-enseki.* ♂ ♀
Let's sit close to the dance floor/bar/band/restrooms/exit/aisle.	***Dansu furoa/bā/bando/*** *otearai;* ***toire****/deguchi/ tsūro -no chikaku-ni suwarō.* ♂ ♀
How many tickets for one drink?	*Nomimono hitotsu-wa* ***chiketto*** *nanmai (desu-ka)?* ♂ ♀
It takes two tickets for one drink.	***Chiketto*** *ni-mai-de nomimono ippai-bun.* ♂ ♀
Free drinks are over there.	***Furī dorinku****-wa asoko.* ♂ ♀
Can we buy beer here?	*Koko-de* ***bīru*** *kaeru?* ♂ ♀
The drinks here taste terrible!	*Koko-no nomimono mazui!* ♀ *Koko-no nomimono mazui-yo!* ♂

This is not very strong.	*Anmari tsuyokunai.* ♂ ♀
They serve weak drinks here.	*Koko-no nomimono minna yowai.* ♂ ♀
Ask for stronger drinks.	*Motto tsuyoi nomimono-o tanonde.**1 ♂ ♀ *Onaji-no-o tsuyokusuru-yō-ni itte.**2 ♂ ♀

*1. Telling your friend that you want your next drink to be stronger.
*2. Telling your friend to order another drink just like you have now, only stronger.

Stronger drinks, please.	*Motto tsuyoi nomimono-o kudasai.* ♂ ♀
Please make this drink stronger.	*Kore motto tsuyokushite kudasai.* ♂ ♀

Let's get some food.	*Tabemono torō.* * ♂ ♀

*From the food bar/counter.

Menu, please.	**Menyū** *kudasai.* ♂ ♀
Have you decided?	*Kimeta?* ♂ ♀
I'll order (for us).	*Atashi-ga ōdā-suru.* ♀ *Boku-ga ōdā-suru.* ♂
I/You forgot the chop-sticks.	*Hashi-o wasureta.* * ♂ ♀

*Fork is *fōku*, knife is **naifu**, and spoon is **supūn**.

I can't decide what to do with my chopsticks.	*Mayoi-bashi.* * ♂ ♀

*For example, you are indecisive when reaching for food, un-sure of what to eat.

NOTE: Food should not be passed from one set of chopsticks to another, for the Japanese place the ashes of their deceased into a funeral urn in this manner. Chopsticks should never be grasped in the fist, since this is how they would be held for use as a weapon. It is considered poor manners to lick chopsticks and extremely offensive to stand chopsticks on end in a bowl of rice, for this is how food is offered to the spirits of the de-ceased.

We need another chair.	*Mō hitotsu isu-ga iru.* ♂ ♀
I'll get that one over there.	*Are mottekuru.* ♂ ♀

I'll bring it with me.	*Motteku.* ♂ ♀
You sit here.	*Koko-ni suwatte.* ♂ ♀
I'll sit there.	*Soko-ni suwaru.* ♂ ♀
Sit by me.	*Atashi-no soba/yoko -ni suwatte.* * ♀ *Boku-no soba/yoko -ni suwatte.* * ♂

*Soba means "close" and *yoko* means "beside."

Sit closer.	*Motto chikaku-ni suwatte.* ♂ ♀
If I get drunk, that's okay.	*Moshi atashi-ga yopparatte-mo heiki-yo.* ♀ *Moshi boku-ga yopparatte-mo heiki-dayo.* ♂

I have a *futon** in my pocket.	***Poketto**-ni futon-ga haitteru.* ♂ ♀

*Japanese bedding. This is a joke, of course.

Will you dance with me?	*Atashi-to odottekureru?* ♀ *Boku-to odottekureru?* ♂
I like to watch you dance.	*Anata-no odori-o mirunoga suki.* ♀ *Kimi-no odori-o mirunoga suki.* ♂
I'm not good at dancing.	***Dansu** umakunai-no.* ♀ ***Dansu** umakunain-da.* ♂
I like slow dancing.	***Surō dansu**-ga suki.* ♂ ♀
Are you in the mood?	*Notteru?** ♂ ♀

*Can be used for any mood.

Not really.	*Anmari.* ♂ ♀ *Betsu-ni.* ♂ ♀
I don't feel like dancing yet.	*Mada odoru-ki shinai.* ♂ ♀
I'm not going to dance yet.	*Mada odoranai.* ♂ ♀
I can't dance to this music.	*Kono kyoku-ja odorenai.* ♂ ♀

I don't know this song.	*Kono uta shiranai.* ♂ ♀
I like rock 'n' roll.	***Rokkun-rōru**-ga suki.* ♂ ♀
I like jazz.	***Jazu**-ga suki.* ♂ ♀
I like American Top-40 music.	***Amerikan Toppu-40**-no ongaku suki.* ♂ ♀
The dance-floor lights are cool.	***Furoa**-no **raito** kakkoii-ne.* ♀ ***Furoa**-no **raito** kakkoii-na.* ♂

Dancing makes me hot.	*Dansu-shitara atsukunatta.* * ♂ ♀

*Hot as in sweaty.

Let's get a breath of fresh air.	*Shinsen-na kūki-o sui-ni ikō.* ♂ ♀
What time do they close?	*Nanji-ni shimaru-no?* ♂ ♀
What time is the last train?	*Saishū densha nanji?* ♂ ♀
What time do you have to be at work?	*Nanji-ni shigoto iku-no?* ♂ ♀
What time is your curfew?	*Mongen nanji?* ♂ ♀
We have plenty of time.	*Jikan-ga tappuri aru.* ♂ ♀
Let's stay to the end.	*Saigo/owari -made iyō.* ♂ ♀
Let's stay till they throw us out.	*Oidasareru-made iyō.* ♂ ♀
Let's go to a coffee shop later.	*Ato-de kōhī shoppu-e ikō.* ♂ ♀
May I see you again?	*Mata aeru?* ♂ ♀
Let's do this again.	*Mata kore shiyō.* ♂ ♀

Let's get together later.	*Ato-de mata-ne.* * ♂ ♀

*This means "Let's separate now and get back together later today."

Let's see each other again.	*Mata aō.* ♂ ♀
Let's meet on Tuesday at your favorite coffee shop.	*Kayōbi-ni anata-no okiniiri-no **kōhī shoppu**-de aō.* ♀ *Kayōbi-ni kimi-no okiniiri-no **kōhī shoppu**-de aō.* ♂
I'm glad we met.	*Aete yokatta.* ♂ ♀
I'm happy to see you again.	*Mata aete ureshii.* ♂ ♀
If I hadn't taken that train, we wouldn't have met.	*Ano densha-ni noranakattara atashitachi awanakatta.* ♀ *Ano densha-ni noranakattara bokutachi awanakatta.* ♂
Do you believe in destiny?	*Unmei-tte shinjiru?* ♂ ♀

PETTING

2

I had a wonderful time last week/last night/ last Friday/yesterday.

Senshū/Kinō-no yoru/Senshū-no kin-yōbi/Kinō -wa tanoshikatta. ♂ ♀

Do you think of me often?

Atashi-no-koto yoku kan-gaeru? ♀
Boku-no-koto yoku kan-gaeru? ♂

I think of you night and day.

Anata-no-koto ichinichi-jū kangaeru. ♀
Kimi-no-koto ichinichi-jū kangaeru. ♂

I couldn't stop thinking about you.

Anata-no-koto bakkari kangaeteta. ♀
Kimi-no-koto bakkari kan-gaeteta. ♂

I remember what you said.

Anata-ga itta-koto oboeteru.* ♀
Kimi-ga itta-koto oboeteru.* ♂

---

*For "remembered," change *oboeteru* to *oboeta.*

I wanted to call you sooner.	*Motto hayaku denwa-shitakatta.* ♂ ♀
What would you like to do tonight?	*Kon-ya nani shitai?* ♂ ♀
What sounds good?	*Nani-ga ii-ka?* ♂ ♀ *Dō-shiyō-ka?* ♂ ♀

NOTE: The boy should make the decision so he doesn't seem weak. The girl will most likely say *Wakannai* ♂ ♀ ("I don't know/care"); *Makaseru-wa* ♀ ("It's up to you"—the boy's equivalent is *Makaseru-yo*); or *Kimete* ♂ ♀ ("You decide").

Can you see me tomorrow?	*Ashita aeru?* * ♂ ♀

*Also means "Can I see you tomorrow?"

Can you go out this Saturday?	*Kondo-no doyōbi derareru?* * ♂ ♀

*This means "Can you go out of the house this Saturday?" Use . . . *dekakerareru?* for "Can you go out with me . . . ?"

I can't wait till then.	*Sore-made matenai.* ♂ ♀
I can wait till then.	*Sore-made materu.* ♂ ♀
I like holding your hand.	*Anata-no te-o nigiru-noga suki.* ♀ *Kimi-no te-o nigiru-noga suki.* ♂
I like kissing you.	*Anata-ni **kissu**-suru-noga suki.* ♀ *Kimi-ni **kissu**-suru-noga suki.* ♂
You're a good kisser.	***Kissu**-ga jōzu-ne.* ♀ ***Kissu**-ga jōzu-dana.* ♂
Your lips are so soft.	*Anata-no kuchibiru-wa totemo yawarakai.* ♀ *Kimi-no kuchibiru-wa totemo yawarakai.* ♂

You're the only one I want.	*Atashi-ga hoshii-nowa anata-dake.* ♀ *Boku-ga hoshii-nowa kimi-dake.* ♂
I can't wait to tell you.	*Iu-noga machikirenai.* ♂ ♀
I was only joking.	*Hon/Tada -no jōdan-dayo.* ♂ ♀
Don't take it so seriously.	*Sonna-ni maji-ni toranaide.* ♀ *Sonna-ni maji-ni toruna-yo.* ♂
It wasn't your day, was it?	*Kyō-wa tsuite-nakatta-nē?* ♀ *Kyō-wa tsuite-nakatta-nā?* ♂
It's boring, isn't it?	*Tsumannai-nē?* ♀ *Tsumannai-nā?* ♂
Do you feel comfortable in public with me?	*Atashi-to hitomae-ni iku-no ki-ni naru?* ♀ *Boku-to hitomae-ni iku-no ki-ni naru?* ♂
I don't want you to get hurt on my account.	*Atashi-no sei-de iya-na omoi sasetakunai.* ♀ *Boku-no sei-de iya-na omoi sasetakunai.* ♂

Tell me when someone talks about us.	*Dareka-ga atashitachi-no-koto hanashitetara oshiete.* ♀ *Dareka-ga bokutachi-no-koto hanashitetara oshiete.* ♂

NOTE: A jealous Japanese boy might make a passing remark to his buddy about a Japanese girl with a foreign boyfriend; some boys might even say something to the girl. Here are a few phrases you might hear.

Who does she think she is?	*Jibun-no-koto nanda-to omotte irun-darō?* ♂
She must like big ones!	*Aitsu ōkii-noga suki nan-daze!* ♂
I wish I had a big one!	*Boku-no-mo motto ōki-kattarana!* * ♂

*This *ōki* only has one *i*.

She has a light butt.	*Shirigaru onna.* * ♂ ♀

*Means she easily hops from boy to boy, bed to bed.

Public restroom.	*Kōshū benjo.* * ♂ ♀

*Means she'll let anyone use her.

She'll be used and then thrown away.	*Yararete suterareru.* * ♂

*To say to the girl, add -yo to *suterareru*. To say to oneself, add -noni to the end of *suterareru*.

She's stupid!	*Aitsu baka-dayo!* ♂
You're dirty! (Your relationship is shameful.)	*Kitanai!* ♂ ♀
Don't be jealous!	*Yakimochi yakuna-yo!** ♂

*This is a good response to any of the above phrases.

Do you care what they think?	*Minna-ga dō omou-ka ki-ni naru?* ♂ ♀
Don't let them bother you.	*Hoka-no-hito-no-koto ki-ni shinaide.* ♀ *Hoka-no-hito-no-koto ki-ni suruna-yo.* ♂
Don't be upset.	*Okoranaide.* ♀ *Okoruna-yo.* ♂

Does your family know about us?	*Anata-no kazoku atashitachi-no-koto shitteru?* ♀ *Kimi-no kazoku bokutachi-no-koto shitteru?* ♂
I told my family about you.	*Kazoku-ni anata-no-koto hanashita.* ♀ *Kazoku-ni kimi-no-koto hanashita.* ♂
Do you think we should see each other again?	*Atashitachi mata atta-hō-ga ii-to omou?* ♀ *Bokutachi mata atta-hō-ga ii-to omou?* ♂

Tell me what you think.	*Anata-wa dō omou-ka oshiete.* ♀
	Kimi-wa dō omou-ka oshiete. ♂
Make it clear.	*Hakkiri-sasete.* ♂ ♀
Please don't go.	*Ikanaide.* ♂ ♀
You don't know.	*Anata-wa shiranai-noyo.* ♀
	Kimi-wa shiranain-da. ♂
We've known each other now for three months.	*Atashitachi shiriatte-kara san-kagetsu-ni naru.* ♀
	Bokutachi shiriatte-kara san-kagetsu-ni naru. ♂
Are you an only child?	*Anata hitorikko?** ♀
	Kimi hitori-musume?* ♂
Are you the oldest?	*Anata ichiban ue?** ♀
	Kimi ichiban ue?* ♂
Are you going to support and provide for your parents in their old age?	*Ryōshin-no rōgo-no mendō miru-no?** ♂ ♀

*Usually the only child or the oldest male will live with his aging parents, supporting and caring for them.

We can make it work.	*Dōnika naru-wayo.* ♀
	Dōnika naru-yo. ♂ ♀

I want to know what you're feeling.

Anata-ga dō omotteru-ka shiritai. ♀
Kimi-ga dō omotteru-ka shiritai. ♂

It'll all change.

Subete kawaru-wayo. ♀
Subete kawaru-yo. ♂ ♀

I can't think of anything but you.

Anata-no-koto igai-wa kangaerarenai. ♀
Kimi-no-koto igai-wa kangaerarenai. ♂

I can't live without your love.

Anata-no ai-nashi-ja ikirarenai. ♀
Kimi-no ai-nashi-ja ikirarenai. ♂

Say you'll be mine.

Atashi-no mono-ni naru-to itte. ♀
Boku-no mono-ni naru-to itte. ♂

I'll make you happy.

Shiawase-ni suru-yo. * ♂

*Girls might think this is a proposal.

I've never felt this way before.

Konna kimochi-ni natta-koto-nai. ♂ ♀

We had fun together, didn't we?

Tanoshikatta-nē? ♀
Tanoshikatta-nā? ♂

Do you remember our first date?	*Hajimete-no dēto oboeteru?* ♂ ♀
Look into my eyes.	*Atashi-no me-o mite.* ♀ *Boku-no me-o mite.* ♂
Stay just a little bit longer.	*Mō chotto-dake issho-ni ite.* ♂ ♀
I couldn't have done it without you.	*Anata-nashi-ja dekinakatta.* ♀ *Kimi-nashi-ja dekinakatta.* ♂

Do Japanese couples go "parking"?	*Nihon-no* **kappuru**-wa **kā-sekkusu**-suru-no?* ♂ ♀

*Kā-sekkusu is car sex.

No. There aren't any good parking places.	*Uun, ii chūsha-basho-ga nai.* ♂ ♀
Where do they go?	*Minna doko-ni iku-no?* ♂ ♀
Let's find a good place.	*Ii basho-o sagasō.* ♂ ♀
How do you know of such a place?	*Sonna basho nande shitteru-no?* ♂ ♀
People can see us here.	*Koko-ja hito-ni miechau-yo.* ♂ ♀
That'll make it more exciting.	*Shigeki-teki-yo.* ♀ *Shigeki-teki-dayo.* ♂
Let's get in the back seat.	**Bakku shīto**-ni suwarō. ♂ ♀
Let's recline the front seats.	**Furonto shīto**-o taosō. ♂ ♀
Take your shoes off.	*Kutsu-o nugi-nayo.* ♂
Relax.	**Rirakkusu**-shite. ♂ ♀
Enjoy yourself.	**Enjoi**-shite. ♂ ♀

Take your _____ off.

Kutsu-o nuide.[1] ♂ ♀
Burajā-*o hazushite.*[2] ♂ ♀
Shitagi-o totte.[3] ♂ ♀
Yōfuku-o nuide.[4] ♂ ♀

[1]. shoes 2. bra 3. underwear 4. clothes

I'm cold.

Samui. ♂ ♀

Make me warm.

Atatamete. ♂ ♀

Doesn't that feel better?

Sono-hō-ga kimochi yokunai? ♂ ♀

Do it like this.

Konna-fū-ni shite. ♂ ♀

That's right.	*Sō-dane.* ♂ ♀
	Sō-dana. ♂
	*Māne.** ♂ ♀

Māne is often used to mean "I know." If said teasingly, it means "Yeah, I know (but I might not tell you)." *Māne* is also used in the jokingly conceited response "Yeah, I know. Don't mention it."

| Let's use the blanket. | *Mōfu-o tsukaō.* ♂ ♀ |

| The blanket's dirty. | *Mōfu kitanai.* ♂ ♀ |

The following are parts of a conversation about sex that anyone might have!

Boy: Let's do it now.	*Ima shiyō.* ♂ ♀
Girl: I want to wait till my wedding night.	*Kekkon-suru-made machitai.* ♂ ♀
Boy: Explain.	*Setsumei-shite.* ♂ ♀
Boy: I want to know why.	*Naze-ka shiritai.* ♂ ♀
Girl: It's too soon.	*Hayasugiru.* ♂ ♀
Girl: The first time should be special.	*Hajimete-no toki-wa tokubetsu-ja nakucha.* ♂ ♀
Girl: It should be more romantic.	*Motto **romanchikku**-ja nakutcha.** ♂ ♀
Girl: Try again next time.	*Kondo tameshite.* ♂ ♀
Boy: What next time?	*Kondo-tte nan-dayo?* ♂
	Kondo-tte nani-yo? ♀
Boy: Now or never!	*Ima-ka mō shinai-ka!* ♂ ♀

Girl: OK, let's go.	*Wakatta, ikō.* ♂ ♀
Boy: Are you sure?	*Honto-ni ii-no?* ♂ ♀
Girl: Hurry, or I'll change my mind.	*Hayaku-shinakya ki-ga kawatchau.* ♀
	Hayaku-shinakya ki-ga kawaru. ♂
Girl: What's wrong?	*Dōka shita-no?** ♂ ♀
	Dō-shita-no?* ♂ ♀
	Nanka atta-no?* ♂ ♀
	Dō-shitan-dayo? ♂

*These should be voiced with some concern.

Boy: This is my first time.	*Kore-ga hajimete-nanda.* ♂
	Kore-ga hajimete-nano. ♀
Boy: I don't know what to do.	*Dō-shitara ii-ka wakannai.* ♂ ♀
Girl: Why not?	*Nande dame-nano?* ♂ ♀
Boy: I haven't read Chapter 3 yet.	*Mada **Chaputā Surii**-o yondenai.* ♂ ♀

MAKING LOVE

3

Stay with me tonight.

Konya-wa atashi-to issho-ni ite. ♀
Konya-wa boku-to issho-ni ite. ♂

I'll tell you something—I love you.

Chotto kiite—aishiteru. ♂♀
Chotto kiite—aishiteru-yo. ♂

I know what's on your mind.

Anata-ga nani kangaeteru-ka shitteru. ♀
Kimi-ga nani kangaeteru-ka shitteru-yo. ♂

No, you don't.

Shiruwakenai-deshō. ♀
Shiruwakenai-darō. ♂

You're thinking dirty thoughts.

Anata-wa yarashii-koto kangaeteru. ♀
Kimi-wa yarashii-koto kangaeteru. ♂

So are you.

Anata-mo. ♀
Kimi-mo. ♂

I like that kind of thinking.	*Sō-yū kangae suki.* ♂ ♀ *Jibun-datte.* * ♂ ♀

*A livelier phrase.

You're the only one I love.	*Anata-dake-o aishiteru.* ♀ *Kimi-dake-o aishiteru.* ♂

NOTE: Go easy at first on the sweet talk. Japanese boys don't throw around a lot of compliments or terms of endearment, so most girls are not accustomed to such attention. However, in the long run, most will definitely enjoy it.

I don't love anyone else.	*Hoka-no dare-mo aishitenai.* ♂ ♀
I love you so much I could die.	*Shinu-hodo aishiteru.* ♂ ♀
I love you for who you are.	*Anata-rashisa-o aishiteru-no.* ♀ *Kimi-rashisa-o aishiterun-da.* ♂

Now is the right time.	*Ima-ga sono-toki-yo.* ♀ *Ima-ga sono-toki-da.* ♂
It hurts to be without you.	*Anata-nashi-da to tsurai.* ♀ *Kimi-nashi-da to tsurai.* ♂
Hold me tight.	*Shikkari dakishimete.* ♀ *Tsuyoku dakishimete.* ♂♀
See me tonight.	*Konya atte.* ♂♀
I don't want to be used.	*Asobaretakunai.** ♂♀

   *Asobu means "to play."

Believe in me. (Trust me.)	*Atashi-o shinjite.* ♀ *Boku-o shinjite.* ♂

I want to know all about you.	*Anata-no-koto subete shiritai.* ♀
	Kimi-no-koto subete shiritai. ♂
You're so very precious.	*Anata-wa tottemo tai-setsu.** ♀
	*Kimi-wa tottemo taise-tsu.** ♂

*This is a very powerful expression of love and devotion. Use with caution.

I want to make love to you.	*Anata-to **beddo-in** shitai.** ♀
	Anata-to netai. ♀
	*Kimi-to **beddo-in** shitai.** ♂
	Kimi-to netai. ♂

Beddo-in means "go to bed." The *in* is pronounced the same as the English "in."

I don't want to go home tonight.	*Konya-wa uchi-ni kaeritakunai.** ♀

*Popular phrase. If she says this, pat yourself on the back.

Do you want to come to my place?	*Uchi-ni kuru?* ♂ ♀
Take me tonight.	*Konya anata-no mono-ni shite.** ♀

*Literally means "Make me yours tonight."

NOTE: Japanese do not often directly say "Let's go to bed." Instead the words are conveyed by the mood. These phrases are useful in case you miss the mood signals. Also, Japanese girls will not be the first to mention going to a love hotel (*rabu hoteru*, a special hotel that rents rooms to couples by the hour) unless they are real playgirls or long-time steadies. And, nice to know, most Japanese girls will not take off their own clothes. Almost always they will wait for the boy to remove them.

It's too early (to go to bed).

Mada hayai. ♂ ♀

Young Japanese people usually live with their parents right up to their wedding day. With small houses and paper-thin walls, the living arrangements are not conducive to good sex. Owning a car provides little escape, for there are few pleasant, obscure places to park short of driving two or three hours to the countryside. So, where do the non-farmers go for a roll in the hay? Better yet, where can you go? Have you heard of a love hotel? No? Come along with us on a trip to a love hotel and we'll show you firsthand this great Japanese institution.

Shall we hail a taxi or drive our car? A car is no problem, for most love hotels have parking facilities that are both free and concealed for those extra-careful people. One would think that the free parking alone would make the love hotel a popular attraction for it exists nowhere else in Japan. Anyway, identifying a love hotel is not so difficult, for most of them are located near big train stations (four tracks or more), in entertainment districts, and along major highways. They are usually well lit with colorful Japanese characters or *katakana* in neon, or just a sign saying "Hotel," with some twinkling stars floating around it. If there are no obvious markings, look for big, big objects on the roof. A 30-foot mock Statue of Liberty or Queen Elizabeth (the ship, not the monarch) on top of a building that has no other visible advertisements or signs is a dead giveaway. Also, the absence of a doorman and furnished lobby with a front desk should scream love hotel.

As we enter the love hotel we see a big display board with pictures of the rooms. Some of the pictures are lighted and some are not; the lighted pictures indicate rooms that are still available. There are many to choose from, all with different themes: hot air balloon, S & M, boxing, and even a race-car room. Let's check out the boxing-ring room. Below the picture is a button which causes the room key to drop out when

pushed. Before we go to the elevator, we notice the two prices below the picture; the cheaper price is the two-hour rate and the other price, usually three to four times higher, is for an all-nighter. Most rooms have yen meters installed to keep you informed of the price you must pay for your pleasure. (Daytime discount rates are available at most love hotels; pack a lunch and enjoy.) At last we arrive at the room. It is identical to that shown in the picture: bed with ropes and stanchions, boxing equipment, refrigerator, TV (regular TV and pay channels), adult videotapes for rent (usually fifteen- or twenty-minute movies), and a large, open shower/bathtub room. Coffee and tea are complimentary, but the sodas and beer are not. "Adult toys" are available; use the menu located next to the phone.

Five hours and three baths later, we leave the room and see two Japanese maids scurry into it to prepare it for the next couple. Before cleaning the room, the maids will thoroughly inventory the refrigerator and all proprietary love notions, including the arched foam pad for the bathroom floor. So, don't put the cap back on the empty bottle and return it to the refrigerator—these cleaning ladies are hip to that skip!

We're back in the lobby again, standing before the pay window. Actually it's not a window but a slit for passing money through. The service at a love hotel is very discreet; you don't see them and they don't see you. ID's aren't even checked. There's a rule of thumb: If you're old enough to pay, you're old enough to play.

Come closer to me.	*Motto chikaku-ni oide-yo.* ♂ ♀
I'm so glad I waited.	*Matte-ite yokatta.* ♂ ♀
Your hair smells good.	*Anata-no kaminoke ii nioi.* ♀ *Kimi-no kaminoke ii nioi.* ♂
What perfume/cologne are you wearing?	*Nanno kōsui/koron tsuketeru-no?* ♂ ♀

What color underwear are you wearing?	*Nani iro-no shitagi-o tsuketeru-no?* ♂ ♀
I like your underwear.	*Sono shitagi kawaii-ne.** ♀
	Sono shitagi kawaii-na.* ♂
	Sono shitagi suteki-ne.* ♀
	Sono shitagi suteki-dana.* ♂

*Kawaii means "cute" and *suteki* means "nice" or "pretty."

That tickles.	*Kusuguttai.* ♂ ♀
	Kusuguttai-yo. ♂
You have beautiful skin.	*Kirei-na hada-dane.* ♂
I found your birthmark.	*Hokuro-o mitsuketa.* ♂ ♀

I'm getting excited.	*Kōfun-shitekichatta.** ♂ ♀

*This phrase is only used for sexual excitement.

I forgot to use protection.	*Hinin-suru-no wasurechatta.* ♂ ♀
Did it hurt?	*Itakatta?* ♂ ♀
When was your first experience?	*Shotaiken itsu?** ♂ ♀
Where was your first experience?	*Shotaiken-wa doko-datta-no?** ♂ ♀

*"Experience" (*taiken*) here means sex.

I won't tell you.	*Oshienai.* ♂ ♀
Do you like to make love in the shower?	**Shawā**-o abinagara **sekkusu**-suru-no suki? ♂ ♀

Do you like to make love in the morning?	*Asa **sekkusu**-suru-no suki?* ♂ ♀
Just joking.	*Jōdan-dayo.* ♂ ♀
I made love.	***Beddo-in** shita.* ♂ ♀
I made love to a girl.	*Onna-o daita.** ♂

*Literally means "I held a girl"—big, bragging words.

breast	*oppai* ♂ ♀ *mune* ♂ ♀
nipple(s)	*chikubi* ♂ ♀
buttocks	***hippu*** ♀ *oshiri* ♂ ♀ *ketsu* ♂
hip	*koshi* ♂ ♀
waist	***uesto*** ♂ ♀
nape of the neck	*kubisuji* ♂ ♀
bellybutton	*oheso* ♂ ♀
ear lobe	*mimitabu* ♂ ♀
down there	*asoko** ♂ ♀

*Asoko usually means "over there" but in this sense it means the "private parts."

NOTE: The Japanese believe a high and big nose on a boy indicates he is well endowed, and a small mouth and skinny ankles on a girl indicate she is tightly endowed.

Bite my shoulders.   *Kata-o kande.* ♂ ♀

NOTE: Japanese boys worry about their virginity and the first time they make love. Normally, Japanese girls will be passive for the first love session so as not to act like experienced lovers.

Sixty-nine.   ***Shikkusu-nain.**** ♂ ♀

*It's "six-nine" in Japanese, not "sixty-nine."

I like to "sixty-nine."   ***Shikkusu-nain*** *suki.* ♂ ♀

Let's do "sixty-nine."   ***Shikkusu-nain****-de shiyō.*
         ♂ ♀

Show me your   *Doko-ga kanjiru-ka*
  erogenous areas.   *oshiete.* ♂ ♀

I like to try different styles.	*Chigau **sutairu**-o tameshitai.* ♂ ♀
You think of a new position.	*Atarashii kakkō-o kangaete.* ♂ ♀
I'm tired of that one.	*Are-niwa akita.* ♂ ♀
That's original.	*Sore-wa **orijinaru**.* ♂ ♀
That sounds exciting.	*Wakuwaku-shichau.* * ♂ ♀ *Wakuwaku-suru.* * ♂ ♀

*Wakuwaku-shichau/suru can be used in nonsexual contexts such as "That party sounds exciting."

Let's do it again.	*Mō ikkai shiyō.* ♂ ♀
girl bottom/boy top	*seijōi** ♂ ♀
boy bottom/girl top	*kijōi** ♂ ♀
doggy style	***bakku**** ♂ ♀

*Seijōi literally means "normal"; *kijōi* means "to ride"; and ***bakku*** means, well, you know. To make a sentence meaning something like "Let's do it doggy style," one would say *Bakku-de shiyō;* for "Let's have the girl ride the hobby horse," one would say *Kijōi-de shiyō;* and for "Let's be missionaries," one would say *Seijōi-de shiyō*.

FIGHTING

4

You told me that you love me, didn't you?

Aishiteru-tte itta-yonē?
♂ ♀
Aishiteru-tte itta-darō? ♂

Are you telling me you don't love me anymore?

Atashi-o mō aishitenai-tte itteru-no? ♀
Boku-o mō aishitenai-tte itteru-no? ♂

You lied to me.

Usotsuita-ne. ♀
Usotsuita-na. ♂

You lie to me all the time.

Itsumo uso-bakkari-tsuku. ♂ ♀

Stop lying to me.

Usotsuku-no yamete. ♂ ♀

It was stupid of me to trust you.

Anata-o shinjiru-nante baka-datta. ♀
Kimi-o shinjiru-nante baka-datta. ♂

I can't trust you anymore.

Anata-no-koto mō shin-jirarenai. ♀
Kimi-no-koto mō shin-jirarenai. ♂

Everything you've said is a lie.

Anata-ga itta-koto minna uso-da. ♀

Kimi-ga itta-koto minna uso-da. ♂

I knew it wouldn't work.

Dame-dato wakatteta-wa. ♀

Dame-dato wakatteta-yo. ♂

You've changed, haven't you?

Anata-wa kawatta-nē? ♀

Kimi-wa kawatta-nā? ♂

You messed up my life.

Atashi-no jinsei-o dame-ni shita. ♀

Boku-no jinsei-o dame-ni shita. ♂

Don't hurt me anymore.	*Mō kizutsukenaide.* ♂ ♀
Let's not tie each other up.	*Otagai-ni shibaru-nowa yameyō.** ♂ ♀

*As in "Let's see other people."

You're the one who said, "Let's stop seeing each other."	*Anata-ga mō au-nowa yosō-tte itta-noyo.* ♀ *Kimi-ga mō au-nowa yosō-tte ittan-dayo.* ♂
Let's not get serious now.	*Ima shinken-ni naru-nowa yosō.** ♂ ♀

*The use of "let's" here is very Japanese, for it invites the other party into the decision-making process. Most Japanese are indirect in their speech. Directly stating one's wishes will halve the normal runaround encountered when talking to Japanese.

I don't want to get serious.	*Shinken-ni naritakunai.* ♂ ♀
I don't even want to think about it.	*Kangae-taku-mo nai.* ♂ ♀

What does that mean?	*Dō-iū imi?* ♂ ♀
Wipe your tears away.	*Namida-o fuite.* ♂ ♀
You take me for granted.	*Atashi-o riyō-shiteru-none.* ♀ *Boku-o riyō-shiterun-da.* ♂
You're so selfish!	*Anata-wa totemo wagamama!* ♀ *Kimi-wa totemo wagama-ma!* ♂
Who am I to you?	*Atashi-wa anata-ni-totte nan-nano?* ♀ *Boku-wa kimi-ni-totte nan-nano?* ♂
Who do you think I am?	*Atashi-o nanda-to omotteru-no?* ♀ *Boku-o nanda-to omotterun-da?* ♂
I wasn't born yesterday.	*Atashi-wa baka-ja nain-dakara.** ♀ *Boku-wa baka-ja nain-dakara.** ♂

*Literally means "I'm not a fool."

I don't belong here.	*Atashi-wa koko-ni awanai.* ♀ *Boku-wa koko-ni awanai.* ♂

Do you know what you're doing?	*Dō-iū tsumori?* ♂ ♀
Don't tell me what to do.	*Meirei-shinaide.* * ♂ ♀
I don't tell you what to do.	*Atashi-wa meirei-shinai-deshō.* * ♀ *Boku-wa meirei-shinai-darō.* * ♂

*Meirei-suru means "to order" and it can be used for anything similar to "Don't order me to . . . "

I'll do whatever I want.	*Atashi-wa atashi-no suki-na-yō-ni suru.* ♀ *Boku-wa boku-no suki-na-yō-ni suru.* ♂
Don't try to change me.	*Atashi-o kaeyō-to-shinaide.* ♀ *Boku-o kaeyō-to shinaide.* ♂

I can't be what you want me to be.	*Anata-ga omotteru-yō-na onna-niwa narenai.* ♀ *Kimi-ga omotteru-yō-na otoko-niwa narenai.* ♂
Let me be me.	*Atashi-no mama-de irasete.* ♀ *Boku-no mama-de irasete.* ♂
Leave me alone.	*Hottoite.* ♂ ♀
What are you doing?	*Nani shiten-no?* ♂ ♀
What the hell are you doing?	*Nani yatten-no?* ♂ ♀
Don't you have something to do?	*Hoka-ni suru-koto-nai-no?* ♂ ♀
Stop following me around.	*Okkakemawasu-nowa yamete.* ♂ ♀
Stop checking up on me.	*Atashi-no-koto shiraberu-nowa yamete.* ♀ *Boku-no-koto shiraberu-nowa yamete.* ♂
Stop troubling me.	*Komarasenaide.* ♂ ♀
I didn't mean to.	*Sonna tsumori-ja nakatta.* ♂ ♀

Don't embarrass me.	*Hazukashii-omoi sasenaide.* ♂ ♀ *Hazukashii-omoi saseruna.* ♂
Don't disappoint me (again).	*(Mō) gakkari-sasenaide.* ♂ ♀ *(Mō) gakkari-saseruna.* ♂
I'm disappointed in you.	*Anata-niwa gakkari-shita.* ♀ *Kimi-niwa gakkari-shita.* ♂
So, what do you want me to say?	*Atashi-ni nante itte hoshii-no?* ♀ *Boku-ni nante itte hoshiin-da?* ♂

Don't pretend nothing happened.

Nani-mo nakatta-yō-na furi-shinaide. ♀
Nani-mo nakatta-yō-na furi-suruna. ♂

How can you act like that (to me)?

Dō-shite sonna taido-o suru-no? ♀
Dō-shite sonna taido-o surun-da? ♂

You made me do it.

Anata-ga atashi-o sō saseta-no. ♀
Kimi-ga boku-o sō sasetan-da. ♂

How many girls have you made cry?

Nannin-no onna-no-ko-o nakasetano? ♀

How many boys have you made cry?

Nannin-no otoko-o nakasetan-da? ♂

Think about the way you treated me!

Anata-ga atashi-o donna-fū-ni atsukatta-ka kangaete mite-yo! ♀
Kimi-ga boku-o donna-fū-ni atsukatta-ka kangaete miro! ♂

Are you playing around with me?

Atashi-no-koto asobi-nano? ♀
Boku-no-koto asobi-nano? ♂

It was just a game.

*Tada-no **gēmu**-datta-no.*
♀
*Tada-no **gēmu**-datta.* ♂

Stop playing these games.

*Gomakasu-nowa
    yamete.** ♂ ♀

*This means something like "Stop trying to hide the truth,"
"Don't change the subject," and "Stop acting like nothing happened" all rolled into one.

Grow up!

Otona-ni natte! ♀
Otona-ni nare! ♂

Don't act like a child.

*Kodomo-mitai-na-koto
    shinaide.* ♂ ♀
*Kodomo-mitai-na-koto
    suruna.* ♂

Act your age.

Toshi-sōō-ni furumatte. ♀
Toshi-sōō-ni furumae-yo.
♂

Don't get too big for
your britches.

Jū-nen hayai. * ♂ ♀

*Literally means "Ten years early."

Stop nagging.

Gocha-gocha iwanaide. *
♀
Gocha-gocha iuna. * ♂

*After the first love session, some Japanese girls will become
very possessive. They'll want to know what you're doing at all
times. Although they were once shy, they'll now act like your
wife—even in public. The following phrases might be needed.

We went to bed only
once.

Ikkai neta-dake-deshō. ♀
Ikkai neta-dake-darō. ♂

Don't act like my wife!

Nyōbō-kidori-suruna! ♂

Don't act like my husband!	*Teishu-zura shinaide!* ♀
Don't act like I'm yours.	*Wagamono-gao shinaide.* ♂ ♀ *Wagamono-gao suruna.* ♂
I'm mad.	*Atama-kichau.* ♀ *Atama-kita.* ♂ *Mukatsuita.* ♂ ♀ *Mukatsuku.* ♂ ♀
Don't make me mad.	*Okorasenaide.* ♀ *Okoraseruna.* ♂
You shouldn't have done that.	*Sonna-koto shinakya yokatta-noni.* ♂ ♀
How dare you!	*Nande sonna-koto dekiru-no!* ♀ *Nande sonna-koto dekirun-da!* ♂
I'm leaving!	*Mō iku!* ♂ ♀ *Mō iku-yo!* ♂
Let me speak frankly.	*Shōjiki-ni iwasete.* ♂ ♀
Do you want me to tell you the truth?	*Honto-no-koto itte hoshii?* ♂ ♀

What you say isn't important.	*Anata-ga iu-koto-wa jūyō-ja naino.* ♀ *Kimi-ga iu-koto-wa jūyō-ja nainda.* ♂
Don't make excuses.	*Iiwake-shinaide.* ♂ ♀ *Iiwake-suruna.* ♂
Don't trick me.	*Damasanaide.* ♂ ♀
I'm tired of you.	*Anata-niwa akita.* ♀ *Kimi-niwa akita.* ♂
Are you tired of me?	*Atashi-ni akita-no?* ♀ *Boku-ni akita-no?* ♂
I'm tired of looking at you.	*Anata-o mi-akita.* ♀ *Kimi-o mi-akita.* ♂
Go look in the mirror!	*Kagami mite denaose-ba!* * ♀ *Kagami mite denaoshi-na!* * ♂

*An English equivalent might be "Look at yourself in the mirror and come back again because *you are ugly!*"

I've had it!	*Mō takusan!* * ♂ ♀

*For extra emphasis stop abruptly on the "*n.*"

I need excitement, not restriction.	*Shigeki-ga hoshii-no, shibararerun-ja nakutte.* ♀

*Shigeki-ga hoshiin-da,
shibararerun-ja
nakutte.* ♂

You don't excite me
anymore.

*Anata-to-dewa shigeki-
teki-ja nai-no.* ♀
*Kimi-to-dewa shigeki-teki-
ja nain-da.* ♂

You aren't any good in
bed.

*Anata-wa **beddo**-de
yokunai.* ♀
*Kimi-wa **beddo**-de
yokunai.* ♂

You're the one!

Jibun-deshō!* ♂ ♀
Jibun-darō!* ♂

*Implying "on the contrary." For example:

Who farted?

Dare-ga onara-shita?
♂ ♀

You did.

Anata/(name) -ga shita. ♀
Kimi/(name) -ga shita. ♂

Wrong!	*Chigau-yo!* ♂ ♀
You're the one!	*Jibun-deshō!* ♂ ♀ *Jibun-darō!* ♂
That's not right!	*Chigau-mon!* ♀ *Chigau-wayo!* ♀ *Chigau-yo!* ♂ ♀
You mean nothing to me.	*Anata-wa atashi-ni-totte nan-no imi-mo nai.* ♀ *Kimi-wa boku-ni-totte nan-no imi-mo nai.* ♂
I'm glad we broke up.	*Wakarete yokkatta.* ♂ ♀
It seems like you're using me.	*Atashi-no-koto riyō shiteru.* ♀ *Boku-no-koto riyō shiteru.* ♂

Pack your stuff and hit the road!	*Nimotsu-o matomete dete-itte!* ♀ *Nimotsu-o matomete dete-ike-yo!* ♂
Give me back the apartment/car key.	***Apāto**/kuruma -no **kii**-o kaeshite.* ♂ ♀
Give me back all the presents I gave to you.	*Atashi-ga ageta **purezento** minna kaeshite.* ♀ *Boku-ga ageta **purezento** minna kaeshite.* ♂
I've already thrown them away.	*Mō sutechatta.* ♂ ♀
Why did you do such a thing?	*Nande sonna-koto shita-no?* ♀ *Nande sonna-koto shitan-dayo?* ♂

I wanted to forget you.	*Anata-no-koto wasuretakatta.* ♀ *Kimi-no-koto wasuretakatta.* ♂
Don't do such a thing.	*Sonna-koto shinaide.* ♂ ♀
Let's talk about this later.	*Sono-koto-wa ato-de hanasō.* ♂ ♀
Let's change the subject.	*Wadai-o kaeyō.* ♂ ♀
Don't change the subject.	*Wadai-o kaenaide.* ♀ *Wadai-o kaeruna.* ♂
(You're such a) worrier.	*Shimpai-chan.* ♂ ♀
(You're such a) crybaby.	*Nakimushi-chan.* ♂ ♀
I'm not your toy.	*Atashi-wa anata-no omocha-ja nai.* ♀ *Boku-wa kimi-no omocha-ja nai.* ♂
Don't think that I'm only yours.	*Atashi-ga anata-dake-no mono-datte omowanaide.* ♀ *Boku-ga kimi-dake-no mono-datte omouna-yo.* ♂

I don't belong to you.	*Atashi-wa anata-no mono-ja nai.* ♀ *Boku-wa kimi-no mono-ja nai.* ♂
Now I'll feel better (because we broke up).	*Kore-de seisei-shita.* * ♂ ♀

*Literally means "Now I'll feel better because of what happened." The "what" can be anything.

You said bad things about me.	*Atashi-no waruguchi-o itta.* ♀ *Boku-no waruguchi-o itta.* ♂

How can you talk to me like that?	*Dō-shite sonna-fū-ni hanaseru-no?* ♀
	Dō-shite sonna-fū-ni hanaserun-dayo? ♂
You talk down to me.	*Anata-wa atashi-o mikudashite hanasu.* ♀
	Kimi-wa boku-o mikudashite hanasu. ♂
You talk to me like I'm a fool.	*Anata-wa atashi-o baka-ni-shite hanasu.* ♀
	Kimi-wa boku-o baka-ni-shite hanasu. ♂
Who cares?	*Dare-ga sonna-koto ki-ni suru-noyo?* ♀
	Dare-ga sonna-koto ki-ni surun-dayo? ♂
I hate you!	*Anata-nanka kirai!* ♀
	Omae-nanka kirai-dayo! ♂
I can find someone better than you.	*Anata-yori ii hito-ga sagaseru.* ♀
	Kimi-yori ii ko-ga sagaseru. ♂
Do it!	*Sure-ba!* ♂ ♀
	Shiro-yo! ♂

Who would want you?	*Dare-ga anata-nanka hoshii-noyo?* ♀ *Dare-ga kimi-nanka hoshii-monka?* ♂
I'm leaving.	*Mō iku.* ♂ ♀
Don't make me laugh.	*Warawasenaide.* ♂ ♀
You're not the only girl in this world.	*Kimi-dake-ga onna-ja nai.* ♂
You're not the only boy in this world.	*Anata-dake-ga otoko-ja nai.* ♀
You can't find anyone better than me.	*Atashi-ijō-no-ko-wa sagasenai-wayo.* ♀ *Boku-ijō-no-yatsu-wa sagasenai-yo.* ♂
I can see whomever I want.	*Atashi-wa atashi-ga aitai hito-ni au-wa.* ♀ *Boku-wa boku-ga aitai hito-ni au-yo.* ♂

Go find yourself a new boyfriend/girlfriend.

*Atarashii **gāru-furendo**-o sagashite.* ♀
*Atarashii **bōi-furendo**-o sagase-yo.* ♂

I've cheated on you.

Anata-o damashiteta-no. ♀
Kimi-o damashitetan-da. ♂

I don't want to believe that.

Shinjitakunai. ♂ ♀

Cheater!/Two-timer!

*Uwaki-mono!** ♂ ♀

*Literally means "Floating mind."

I have another boyfriend/girlfriend.

*Atashi-wa hoka-ni **bōi-furendo**-ga iru.* ♀
*Boku-wa hoka-ni **gāru-furendo**-ga iru.* ♂

I've tried to tell you many times, but I couldn't.

Nando-mo iō-to shita-kedo. ♂ ♀

I know you're seeing another person.

Futamata kaketeru-no shitteru-wa. ♀
Futamata kaketeru-no shitteru-yo. ♂

I know how you look at other girls.

Anata-ga donna-fū-ni hoka-no-ko-o miteru-ka shitteru-wa. ♀

I know how you look at other boys.

Kimi-ga donna-fū-ni hoka-no-otoko-o miteru-ka shitteru-yo. ♂

I love someone else.

Hoka-ni suki-na hito-ga iru-no. ♀
Hoka-ni suki-na hito-ga irun-da. ♂

I saw you with another boy.

Kimi-ga hoka-no-otoko-to iru-no-o mita. ♂

I saw you with another girl.	*Anata-ga hoka-no-ko-to iru-no-o mita.* ♀
What kind of a girl is she?	*Ano-ko dare?* ♂ ♀
What kind of a boy is he?	*Ano hito dare?* ♂ ♀
I won't forgive you.	*Anata-no-koto yurusanai.* ♀ *Kimi-no-koto yurusanai.* ♂
You'd better believe that.	*Shinjita-hō-ga ii-yo.* ♂ ♀
Be nice to your new sweetheart.	*Atarashii koibito-ni yasashiku-ne.* ♀ *Atarashii koibito-ni yasashiku-na.* ♂

Don't make her/him sad.	*Kanojo/Kare -o kanashi-mase-naide.* ♂ ♀
I believed in you, yet you tricked me.	*Anata-o shinjiteta-noni damashita.* ♀ *Kimi-o shinjiteta-noni damashita.* ♂
Let me explain.	*Setsumei-sasete.* ♂ ♀
Please listen to me.	*Dōka kiite.* ♂ ♀
Choose: him or me.	*Boku-ka kare-ka erande.* ♂
Choose: her or me.	*Atashi-ka kanojo-ka erande.* ♀
Have you already decided which one?	*Dotchi-ni suru-ka kimeta?* ♂ ♀
Don't make promises you can't keep.	*Mamorenai yakusoku-wa shinaide.* ♂ ♀
I can't stand it.	*Gaman-dekinai.* ♂ ♀
It happens all the time.	*Itsumo sō-nano.* ♀ *Itsumo sō-nanda.* ♂
You forget everything.	*Anata-wa nandemo wasurechau.* ♀ *Kimi-wa nandemo wasureru.* ♂

Have you forgotten so soon?	*Sonna-ni hayaku wasurechatta-no?* ♀ *Sonna-ni hayaku wasureta-no?* ♂
You forgot my birthday.	*Anata-wa atashi-no tanjōbi wasureta.* ♀ *Kimi-wa boku-no tanjōbi wasureta.* ♂
You forgot our anniversary.	*Anata-wa atashitachi-no kinenbi wasureta.* ♀ *Kimi-wa bokutachi-no kinenbi wasureta.* ♂
You never came over.	*Anata-wa konakatta.* ♀ *Kimi-wa konakatta.* ♂
You left me at _____.	*Anata-wa atashi-o _____-ni oitetta.* ♀ *Kimi-wa boku-o _____-ni oitetta.* ♂
You left me (stranded).	*Anata-wa atashi-o oitetta.* ♀ *Kimi-wa boku-o oitetta.* ♂
You left without telling me.	*Nani-mo iwanaide itchatta.* ♂ ♀
What a coincidence seeing you here.	*Konna tokoro-de au-nante.* ♂ ♀

I was just about to call you.	*Anata-ni denwa-suru-tokoro-datta.* ♀ *Kimi-ni denwa-suru-tokoro-datta.* ♂
I tried to call you.	*Anata-ni denwa-shita-noyo.* ♀ *Kimi-ni denwa-shitan-dayo.* ♂
Why didn't you call me?	*Nande denwa-kurenakatta-no?* ♂ ♀
I was busy.	*Isogashikatta.* ♂ ♀
I didn't have ten yen.	*Jū-en-ga nakatta.* ♂ ♀

I waited all night for your call.	*Hitoban-jū denwa-o matteta.* ♂ ♀
You never called.	*Denwa-o kurenakatta.* ♂ ♀
Where were you?	*Doko-ni ita-no?* ♂ ♀
That's a secret!	*Himitsu-yo!* ♀ *Himitsu-dayo!* ♂
I don't play around.	*Atashi-wa asobanai.* ♀ *Boku-wa asobanai.* ♂
I was busy playing around.	*Asobimakutteta.* ♂ ♀
Don't do that again.	*Mō sonna-koto shinaide.* ♂ ♀
I'll forget about it.	*Mō sono-koto-wa wasureru-wa.* ♀ *Mō sono-koto-wa wasureru-yo.* ♂
I'm not mad anymore.	*Mō okottenai-wa.* ♀ *Mō okottenai-yo.* ♂
Are you still mad?	*Mada okotteru?* ♂ ♀
You're still mad, aren't you?	*Mada okotteru-deshō?* ♀ *Mada okotteru-darō?* ♂

I think I was wrong.	*Atashi-ga machigatteta-to omou.* ♀
	Boku-ga machigatteta-to omou. ♂
I shouldn't have done that.	*Sō shinakya yokatta.* ♀
	Sō surun-ja nakatta. ♂ ♀
I don't know why I did that.	*Dō-shite sō shita-noka wakannai.* ♂ ♀
I think I was too excited.	*Kōfun-shisugiteta.* ♂ ♀
I think I was too nervous.	*Ira-ira-shiteta.* ♂ ♀
I was out of my mind.	*Ki-ga chigatteta.* ♂ ♀
It was silly of me (to do that).	*Atashi-ga baka-datta.* ♀
	Boku-ga baka-datta. ♂

You have so much more than they do.	*Anata-wa minna-ga mottenai mono-o motteru.* ♀ *Kimi-wa minna-ga mottenai mono-o motteru.* ♂
If you change your mind, let me know.	*Moshi ki-ga kawattara oshiete.* ♂ ♀
What changed your mind?	*Nani-ga anata-no kangae-o kaeta-no?* ♀ *Nani-ga kimi-no kangae-o kaeta-no?* ♂
I didn't mean to hurt you.	*Kizutsukeru tsumori-wa nakatta.* ♂ ♀
I should've thought about it more.	*Motto kangaereba yokatta.* ♂ ♀

I hurt your feelings, didn't I?	*Ki-ni sawatta-deshō?* ♀ *Ki-ni sawatta-darō?* ♂
I know I hurt your feelings.	*Anata-no-koto kizutsuketa-ne.* ♀ *Kimi-no-koto kizutsuketa-na.* ♂
I'll do anything to make you forgive me.	*Yurushite-morau-tame-nara nandemo suru-wa.* ♀ *Yurushite-morau-tame-nara nandemo suru-yo.* ♂
Anything?	*Nandemo?* ♂ ♀
I was blind to the truth.	*Shinjitsu-ga mietenakatta.* ♂ ♀
You should understand how I feel.	*Atashi-ga donna omoi-datta-ka wakatte-yo.* ♀ *Boku-ga donna omoi-datta-ka wakatte-kure.* ♂
You didn't even listen to me.	*Kiitekuresae-mo shinakatta.* ♂ ♀
I didn't mean to.	*Sonna tsumori-ja nakatta.* ♂ ♀
Let's get back together.	*Nakanaori-shiyō.* ♂ ♀

Promise it will never happen again.	*Mō nido-to okoranai-tte yakusoku-shite.* ♂ ♀
I promise.	*Yakusoku-suru.* ♂ ♀
I wish I hadn't done such a thing.	*Anna-koto shinakereba yokatta.* ♂ ♀
Please take me back.	*Yori-o modoshite.* ♂ ♀
I'm always doing silly things.	*Atashi-tte itsumo baka-na-koto suru-ne.* ♀ *Boku-tte itsumo baka-na-koto suru-na.* ♂
I feel so lonely.	*Samishii-no.* ♀ *Samishiin-da.* ♂
I'm losing sleep.	*Nemurenai-no.* ♀ *Nemurenain-da.* ♂
You were the first and you'll be the last.	*Anata-ga hajimete-de, saigo-yo.* ♀ *Kimi-ga hajimete-de, saigo-da.* ♂
Whenever you need someone, I'll always be there.	*Dare-ka hitsuyō-na toki atashi-ga itsumo iru-wa.* ♀ *Dare-ka hitsuyō-na toki boku-ga itsumo iru-yo.* ♂

Whatever you want I'll give it to you.	*Nandemo hoshii mono ageru.* ♂ ♀
Come back to me.	*Atashi-no-toko-ni modotte.* ♀ *Boku-no-toko-ni modotte.* ♂
I believe you still love me.	*Mada aishitekureteru-tte shinji-teru.* ♂ ♀
Don't throw away this chance.	*Kono **chansu** nogasanaide.* ♂ ♀
It might be your last.	*Saigo-kamo shirenai.* ♂ ♀

Don't be sad.	*Kanashimanaide.* ♂ ♀
Cheer up.	*Genki dashite.* ♂ ♀
Don't worry; be happy.	*Shinpai-shinaide, akarukushite.* ♂ ♀
I can't give her/him up.	*Kanojo/Kare -o akiramerarenai.* ♂ ♀
I can't forget her/him.	*Kanojo/Kare -o wasurerarenai.* ♂ ♀

MARRIAGE

5

When do you want to get married?

Itsu kekkon-shitai? * ♂ ♀

At what age do you want to marry?

Nansai-de kekkon-shitai? * ♂ ♀

Are you going to work after you're married?

Kekkon-shita-ato hataraku tsumori? * ♂ ♀

Do you think you're ready to get married?

Kekkon-suru junbi-wa dekiteru? * ♂ ♀

*These are "beating around the bush" questions to ensure it's OK to ask the big question.

Are you Christian or Buddhist?

Kurisuchan *soretomo Bukkyō?* ♂ ♀

Why all these questions about marriage?

Nande kekkon-no-koto bakkari kiku-no? ♂ ♀

Stop beating around the bush!

Gucha-gucha iwanaide! ♂ ♀

Are you trying to propose to me?

Puropōzu-*shiyō-to shiteru-no?* ♂ ♀

What's the question?	*Nani-ga kikitai-no?* ♂ ♀
What's the answer?	*Kotae-wa?* ♂ ♀
What's on your mind?	*Nani-o kangaeteru-no?* ♂ ♀
Will you marry me?	*Kekkon-shitekureru?* ♂ ♀
Will you use my last name?	*Boku-no myōji-o tsukat-tekureru?** ♂
Shall we share the rest of our lives together?	*Nokori-no jinsei-o issho-ni sugosanai?** ♂ ♀
Will you make my *miso* soup for breakfast?	*Chōshoku-no miso-shiru-o tsukuttekureru?** ♂
Will you have my baby?	*Boku-no kodomo-o undekureru?** ♂

*The above phrases are "Will you marry me?" substitutes. *Miso* soup is made from soybean paste. It can be eaten at any meal but is an important item in a traditional Japanese breakfast.

I can't marry you.	*Anata-to kekkon-dekinai.* ♀ *Kimi-to kekkon-dekinai.* ♂
I don't want to marry you.	*Anata-to kekkon-shitakunai.* ♀ *Kimi-to kekkon-shitakunai.* ♂

I can't get married now.	*Ima kekkon-dekinai.* ♂ ♀
Why not?	*Nande dame-nano?** ♂ ♀

*Go back to Chapter 4 to continue this conversation.

I have some good news to tell you.	*Ii **nyūsu** arun-da.* ♂ ♀
I can't tell you on the phone.	*Denwa-ja ienai.* ♂ ♀
You're going to be a daddy!	*Anata-wa **papa**-ni naru-noyo!* ♀

I'm pregnant.	*Atashi ninshin shiteru-no.* ♀
Congratulations!	*Omedetō!* ♂ ♀
Are you sure?	*Honto-ni?* ♂ ♀
I haven't had my period yet.	*Seiri-ga konai-no.* ♀
When was your last period?	*Saigo-no seiri-wa itsu atta-no?* ♂ ♀
When did you find that out?	*Itsu sore-ga wakatta-no?* ♂ ♀
Why didn't you tell me sooner?	*Nande motto hayaku iwanakatta-no?* ♂ ♀
I've been wanting to tell you, but (I didn't).	*Iitakatta-kedo . . .* ♂ ♀
What month are you now?	*Ima nankagetsu?* ♂ ♀
When's the baby due?	*Yoteibi-wa itsu?* ♂ ♀
It's going to change our lives.	*Atashitachi-no jinsei-o kaeru.* * ♀ *Bokutachi-no jinsei-o kaeru.* * ♂

*Remove the *tachi* to say "It's going to change my life."

I want a boy/girl.	*Otoko-no-ko/Onna-no-ko-ga hoshii.* ♂ ♀
It's our destiny.	*Kore-ga atashitachi-no unmei.* ♀ *Kore-ga bokutachi-no unmei.* ♂
There's no better news than this.	*Kore-ijō ii* **nyūsu**-*wa nai-yo.* ♂ ♀
When will your stomach show?	*Itsu-goro-kara onaka-ga medachi-hajimeru-no?* ♂ ♀

Take good care of
  yourself.

*Karada-ni yoku ki-o
  tsukete.* ♂

Start reading books
  about babies.

*Akachan-ni-tsuite-no hon-
  o yomi-hajime-nayo.* ♂

We should think of a
  name.

*Namae-o kangae-
  nakucha.* ♂ ♀

Maybe it was too early to
  take the test.

***Tesuto**-o ukeru-niwa
  hayasugirun-janai.* ♂ ♀

Take the test again.

*Mō ichido **tesuto**-o ukete.*
  ♂ ♀

Are you sure it's mine?

Hontō-ni boku-no-ko? ♂

I won't answer that!

Kotaenai-wa! ♀
Kotaenai-yo! ♂

I guess that our protection wasn't good enough.	*Hinin-ga jūbun-ja nakattan-dane.* ♂ ♀
You said it was safe.	*Hinin shiteru-tte itta-janai.* ♀ *Hinin shiteru-tte itta-darō.* ♂
I can't be held responsible.	*Sekinin torenai.* ♂ ♀
Don't run away from your responsibility.	*Sekinin-nogare shinaide.* ♂ ♀
Accept the responsibility.	*Sekinin-o totte.* ♂ ♀
See you later.	*Ato-de-ne.* ♂ ♀ *Ato-de-na.* ♂
Don't call me.	*Denwa-shinaide.* ♂ ♀
I'll call you later.	*Atashi-ga ato-de denwa-suru.* ♀ *Boku-ga ato-de denwa-suru.* ♂
It's a bad time.	*Jiki-ga warui.* ♂ ♀
It's too early.	*Hayasugiru.* ♂ ♀
It's your fault.	*Anata-no sei.* ♀ *Kimi-no sei.* ♂

What will happen to us? · *Atashitachi dō narun-deshō?* ♀

Bokutachi dō narun-darō? ♂

I want to keep the baby. · *Akachan-o umitai.* * ♀

*Literally means "I want to deliver the baby."

It's our baby. · *Atashitachi-no akachan-yo.* ♀

Bokutachi-no akachan-dayo. ♂

What do you think? · *Dō omou?* ♂ ♀

Let's have the operation. · *Shujutsu-o shiyō.* ♂ ♀

You're such a cold person! · *Anata-tte hontō-ni tsumetai-none!* ♀

Kimi-tte hontō-ni tsumetai-na! ♂

I can't kill our baby. · *Atashitachi-no akachan-o korosenai.* ♀

Bokutachi-no akachan-o korosenai. ♂

I can't do that. · *Sonna-koto dekinai.* ♂ ♀

We don't have a choice. · *Sonna-koto itterarenai.* ♂ ♀

We're not ready yet. · *Mada hayai.* ♂ ♀

Let's raise the baby.

Akachan-o sodate-yō.
♂ ♀

I don't need your help.

*Anata-no tasuke-wa
  iranai.* ♀
Kimi-no tasuke-wa iranai.
  ♂

You'll be sorry.

Kōkai-suru-yo. ♂ ♀

Please give it up this
  time.

Konkai-wa akiramete.
  ♂ ♀

We have to think about it carefully.	*Yoku kangaenakucha.* ♂ ♀
I'll pay for it.	*Atashi-ga harau.* ♀ *Boku-ga harau.* ♂
How much does it cost?	*Ikura kakaru?* ♂ ♀
Do you have that much money?	*Sore-dake okane motteru?* ♂ ♀
I don't make enough money.	*Sonna-ni okane-o kaseganai.* ♂ ♀
I'll make the money for it.	*Okane-o tsukuru-wa.* ♀ *Okane-o tsukuru-yo.* ♂
I can get it.	*Te-ni hairu-yo.* ♂ ♀
It's impossible to have a baby now.	*Ima akachan-o motsu-nowa muri-yo.* ♀ *Ima akachan-o motsu-nowa muri-dayo.* ♂
What do we do now?	*Dō-suru?* ♂ ♀
I'm scared.	*Kowai-wa.* ♀
Will you go with me?	*Atashi-to issho-ni ittekureru?** ♀

*As in "Will you accompany me?"

Do you have to stay in the hospital overnight?	*Byōin-ni ippaku shinakucha ikenai-no?* ♂ ♀
Is there anything I can do for you?	*Nanika atashi-ni dekiru-koto aru?* ♀ *Nanika boku-ni dekiru-koto aru?* ♂
We'll be able to have a baby another time.	*Mata itsuka akachan-o moteru-yo.* ♂ ♀
I wish it were a dream.	*Yume-dattara yokatta-noni.* ♂ ♀
I don't know what to do.	*Dō-shitara ii-ka wakannai.* ♂ ♀
It's up to you.	*Anata-ni makaseru.* ♀ *Kimi-ni makaseru.* ♂

You decide.

Anata-ga kimete. ♀
Kimi-ga kimete. ♂

Let me think it over.

Mō ichido kangae-sasete. ♂ ♀

Whatever you want to do will be fine with me.

Anata-ga shitai-yō-ni shite-ii-yo. ♀
Kimi-ga shitai-yō-ni shite-ii-yo. ♂

The child is ours, not just mine.

Akachan-wa atashi-dake-no mono-ja nai-yo. ♀
Akachan-wa boku-dake-no mono-ja nai-yo. ♂

You knew it could happen, didn't you?

Kō-naru-kamo shirenai-tte wakattetan-deshō? ♀
Kō-naru-kamo shirenai-tte wakattetan-darō? ♂

Let's decide together.

Issho-ni kimeyō. ♂ ♀

I should tell my parents.

Ryōshin-ni iwanakucha. ♂ ♀

I should call my parents.

Ryōshin-ni denwa-shinakucha. ♂ ♀

What will your parents think?

Anata-no ryōshin dō omou-kana? ♀
Kimi-no ryōshin dō omou-darō? ♂

I already told my parents.	*Mō ryōshin-ni itta.* ♂ ♀
What did they say?	*Nante itteta?* ♂ ♀
Were they mad?	*Okotteta?* ♂ ♀
Are your parents on our side?	*Anata-no ryōshin atashitachi-no mikata?* ♀ *Kimi-no ryōshin bokutachi-no mikata?* ♂
Will your parents help us?	*Anata-no ryōshin tasuketekureru-kana?* ♀ *Kimi-no ryōshin tasuketekureru-kana?* ♂

Let me meet your parents.

Anata-no ryōshin-ni awa-sete. ♀
Kimi-no ryōshin-ni awa-sete. ♂

Introduce me to your family.

Anata-no kazoku-ni shōkai-shite. ♀
Kimi-no kazoku-ni shōkai-shite. ♂

Now is not a good time.

Ima-wa yokunai. ♂ ♀

Maybe I shouldn't meet your parents now.

Tabun ima anata-no ryōshin-ni awanai-hō-ga ii. ♀
Tabun ima kimi-no ryōshin-ni awanai-hō-ga ii. ♂

Now is as good a time as any.

Itsu-datte onaji-yo. ♀
Itsu-datte onaji-dayo. ♂

I'll meet your parents as soon as possible.	*Dekiru-dake hayaku anata-no ryōshin-ni au.* ♀ *Dekiru-dake hayaku kimi-no ryōshin-ni au.* ♂
Do you think your parents will accept our baby/marriage?	*Anata-no ryōshin atashitachi-no akachan/kekkon -o mitomete-kureru-kana?* ♀ *Kimi-no ryōshin bokutachi-no akachan/ kekkon -o mitomete-kureru-kana?* ♂
We can live with my parents for a while.	*Atashi-no ryōshin-to shibaraku issho-ni sumeru-wa.* ♀ *Boku-no ryōshin-to shibaraku issho-ni sumeru-yo.* ♂
How long is "a while"?	*Shibaraku-tte dono gurai?* ♂ ♀
What are you going to do about your job/school?	*Shigoto/Gakkō -o dō-suru tsumori?* ♂ ♀
Are you going to quit work/school?	*Shigoto/Gakkō -o yameru tsumori?* ♂ ♀

I should get a better paying job.	*Motto kyūryō-no ii shigoto-o sagasanakucha.* ♂ ♀
I'd better get a second job.	*Arubaito-o shita-hō-ga ii-ne.* ♀ *Arubaito-o shita-hō-ga ii-na.* ♂
I don't want my wife to work.	*Boku-no kanojo*-niwa hataraite hoshikunai.* ♂

*Kanojo in this case means "wife."

We have to hurry to have the wedding.	*Isoide kekkon-shiki-o agenakucha.* ♂ ♀
Do you cook often?	*Yoku ryōri-suru?* ♂ ♀

I'd like to try your home cooking.

Anata-no teryōri-ga tabetai. ♀
Kimi-no teryōri-ga tabetai. ♂

What's your best dish?

Tokui-ryōri-wa nani? ♂ ♀

I want to try that.

Sore-o tabete-mitai. ♂ ♀

Are your parents fat?

Anata-no ryōshin futtoteru? ♀
Kimi-no ryōshin futtoteru? ♂

Don't worry.

Shinpai-shinaide. ♂ ♀

I'm sure the neighbors will talk about us.

Kinjo-no-hitotachi atashitachi-no-koto hanasu-ne. ♀
Kinjo-no-hitotachi bokutachi-no-koto hanasu-darō. ♂

Are you worried about what your neighbors might say?

Kinjo-no-hito-ga nante iu-ka ki-ni naru? ♂ ♀

Does your family care what they say?

Karera-ga iu-koto anata-no kazoku ki-ni suru? ♀
Karera-ga iu-koto kimi-no kazoku ki-ni suru? ♂

Tell me what to do in front of your family.	*Anata-no kazoku-no mae-de dō-shitara ii-ka oshiete.* ♀ *Kimi-no kazoku-no mae-de dō-shitara ii-ka oshiete.* ♂

NOTE: You shouldn't kiss or hug in front of a girl's family until they know you really well. It's OK to hold hands though.

What should I talk about?	*Nani-o hanaseba ii?* ♂ ♀
What shall I bring?	*Nani-o motte-ikō-ka?* ♂ ♀
Tell me what to say.	*Nanika iu-koto oshiete.* ♂ ♀
Do you think your family will like me?	*Anata-no kazoku atashi-no-koto ki-ni itte-kureru-kana?* ♀ *Kimi-no kazoku boku-no-koto ki-ni itte-kureru-kana?* ♂
Does your father smoke?	*Anata-no otōsan **tabako** suu?* ♀ *Kimi-no otōsan **tabako** suu?* ♂
Does your father drink?	*Anata-no otōsan osake nomu?* ♀ *Kimi-no otōsan osake nomu?* ♂

What's your father's hobby/work?

Otōsan-no shumi/shigoto -wa nani? ♂ ♀

*Typical hobbies are: *shōgi*, Japanese chess; *tsuri*, fishing; **gorufu**, golf; *keiba*, horse racing, which means "betting on horses"; and *pachinko*, a pinball-style game, actually more of an addiction than a hobby.

What's your father proud of?

Anata-no otōsan nani-o hokori-ni shiteru? ♀
Kimi-no otōsan nani-o hokori-ni shiteru? ♂

Who will like me the most?

Dare-ga atashi-o ichiban ki-ni itte-kureru-kana? ♀
Dare-ga boku-o ichiban ki-ni itte-kureru-kana? ♂

Who will oppose our marriage?	*Dare-ga atashitachi-no kekkon hantai-suru-kana?* ♀
	Dare-ga bokutachi-no kekkon hantai-suru-kana? ♂
Who will support our marriage?	*Dare-ga atashitachi-no kekkon ōen shitekureru-kana?* ♀
	Dare-ga bokutachi-no kekkon ōen-shitekureru-kana? ♂
Is anyone on my side?	*Dare-ka atashi-no mikata iru?* ♀
	Dare-ka boku-no mikata iru? ♂
Maybe some other time.	*Tabun chigau-hi.* ♂ ♀
We can do it later.	*Ato-de dekiru.* ♂ ♀
How much will the wedding cost?	*Kekkon-shiki-no hiyō ikura kakaru?* ♂ ♀
How much will your parents pay?	*Anata-no ryōshin ikura dashite-kureru?* ♀
	Kimi-no ryōshin ikura dashite-kureru? ♂
We should begin preparing now.	*Ima-kara yōi-shita-hō-ga ii.* ♂ ♀

Should we have a Japa-
nese- or an American-
style wedding?

*Amerika-shiki-to Nihon-
shiki-to dotchi-ni suru?*
♂ ♀

What's the difference?

Nani-ga chigau-no? ♂ ♀

A Japanese-style wedding is performed by a *Shinto*
priest and the wedding ceremony guests are limited to
the family. Conversely, an American-style wedding in
Japan is performed by a clergyman from any of the
Christian denominations and the guests include both
family and friends. Both bride and groom usually wear
kimono for a Japanese-style wedding ceremony,
whereas a wedding dress and a tuxedo are worn for
an American-style wedding. A dinner party follows
both ceremonies, in which a full-course dinner is
served to the wedding party and guests as friends

and relatives take turns giving speeches and singing songs. In a modest wedding, the bride will wear the same wedding dress throughout the dinner party, but she might change her hairstyle. For a more elaborate wedding, the bride might change her clothes twice during the dinner party alone. The following factors determine the cost of the wedding: how many guests are invited (which will determine the number of presents that are to be given to the guests and the number of dinner settings), what is served for dinner, how many times the bride changes clothes, and the location of the wedding hall. Incidentally, in Japan the wedding hall takes care of everything; you walk in single and leave married.

HEALTH

6

You have a nice figure.	*Sutairu-ga ii-ne.* ♀ *Sutairu-ga ii-na.* ♂
You're slim.	*Yaseteru-ne.* ♀ *Yaseteru-na.* ♂ *Surimu-dane.* ♀ *Surimu-dana.* ♂
Did you lose weight?	*Yaseta?* ♂ ♀
Did you gain weight?	*Futtota?* ♂ ♀
Do you think I need to diet?	*Daietto-shita-hō-ga ii-to omou?* ♂ ♀
No, I like the way you are now.	*Uun, sono-mama-no anata-ga suki.* ♀ *Uun, sono-mama-no kimi-ga suki.* ♂
You need to be on a diet.	*Daietto-shita-hō-ga ii-yo.* ♂ ♀
You should stop smoking.	*Tabako yame-nayo.* ♂ ♀

Stop smoking.	***Tabako** yamete.* ♂ ♀
Smoking is not good for your health.	***Tabako**-wa karada-ni yokunai.* ♂ ♀
You need to exercise.	***Ekisasaizu**-shita-hōga ii-yo.* ♂ ♀
Do you exercise?	***Ekisasaizu** suru?* ♂ ♀
Do you like to exercise?	***Ekisasaizu** suki?* ♂ ♀
We can exercise together.	***Ekisasaizu** issho-ni dekiru-yo.* ♂ ♀
What type of exercises do you do?	*Donna **ekisasaizu**-suru-no?* ♂ ♀
I run three kilometers every day.	*Mainichi san-**kiro** hashiru.* ♂ ♀
I go to the gym.	***Jimu**-ni iku.* ♂ ♀

I go to the pool.	*Pūru-ni iku.* ♂ ♀
I like to swim.	*Oyogu-noga suki.* ♂ ♀

NOTE: After a good exercise session, say *Koshi-ga itai,* which means "My back hurts." People listening to you will really think you had some good sex last night and that is the reason for your backache.

I'm a vegetarian.	*Saishoku-shugi desu.* ♂ ♀
	Atashi **bejitarian.** ♀
	Boku **bejitarian.** ♂
I don't eat fried food.	*Agemono-wa tabenai.* ♂ ♀
I can't live without McDonalds.	*Makudonarudo nashi-ja ikirarenai.* ♂ ♀

QUICK-GUIDES

Lover's

GUIDE
TO
JAPAN

*Where the Action Is . . .
and How to Get Some!*

Boye De Mente

ISBN 0-8048-1589-5

YENBOOKS

Yoshiwara

The Pleasure Quarters of Old Tokyo

吉原

by Stephen and
Ethel Longstreet

ISBN 0-8048-1599-2

Also from **YENBOOKS**

" Informative . . . insightful . . . outrageous."
—Boye De Mente

The Truth About Japan!

Selected and edited by **Andrew Watt**

ISBN 0-8048-1562-3